OFFICIAL

FORTNITE

THE ULTIMATE
TRIVIA BOOK

First published in the UK in 2020 by WILDFIRE an imprint
of HEADLINE PUBLISHING GROUP

Paperback 978 14722 8005 3

Design by Amazing 15
All images © Epic Games, Inc.

Printed and bound in Great Britain by Clays Ltd, Elcograf S.P.A

Every effort has been made to fulfil requirements with regard to reproducing copyright material.
The author and publisher will be glad to rectify any omissions at the earliest opportunity. Headline's
policy is to use papers that are natural, renewable and recyclable products and made from wood
grown in sustainable forests. The logging and manufacturing processes are expected to conform to
the environmental regulations of the country of origin.

HEADLINE PUBLISHING GROUP
An Hachette UK Company
Carmelite House
50 Victoria Embankment
London, EC4 0DZ
www.headline.co.uk www.hachette.co.uk

Little, Brown and Company
Hachette Book Group
1290 Avenue of the Americas, New York, NY 10104

Visit us at hbgusa.com/Fortnite
www.epicgames.com

First Edition: August 2020 • First U.S. Edition: April 2021

ISBNs: 978-0-316-28555-1 (pbk.), 978-0-316-28615-2 (ebook)

U.S. edition printed in the United States of America

All images © Epic Games, Inc.

LSC-C
Printing 1, 2021

OFFICIAL
FORTNITE
THE ULTIMATE
TRIVIA BOOK

Little, Brown and Company
New York   Boston

CONTENTS

TEST YOUR BATTLE ROYALE BRAIN!

Wanna take a full-on Fortnite trivia test? If you're clued in on Outfits, Emotes, seasons, LTMs, locations, Weapons, and everything else Battle Royale-related, then the official *Fortnite: The Ultimate Trivia Book* is perfect for you!

These 350 questions are split into Common, Uncommon, Rare, Epic, and Legendary sections to push you to the limit. Accept the challenge, because it's time to take your Fortnite trivia knowledge to the next level. The vast range of exciting multiple-choice questions will have you scratching your head, but whether you're an experienced Battle Royale pro or new to the Island, take on the quiz quest and see what you score.

YOUR FORTNITE TRIVIA TEST STARTS HERE—GOOD LUCK!

FORTNITE
TRIVIA
COMMON

1 WHO IS THE LEADER OF THE AGENCY?

- [ ] **A.** Agent Peely
- [ ] **B.** Midas
- [ ] **C.** Meowscles

2 WHICH OF THESE IS NOT A CLASS OF WEAPONS?

- [ ] **A.** Unobtainable
- [ ] **B.** Rare
- [ ] **C.** Legendary

3 WHAT COLOR IS THE TRADITIONAL SUPPLY DROP CRATE?

- [ ] **A.** Blue
- [ ] **B.** Yellow
- [ ] **C.** Green

4 IN WHICH SEASON WAS TILTED TOWERS FIRST ADDED?

- [ ] **A.** Season 5
- [ ] **B.** Season 1
- [ ] **C.** Season 2

5 GETTING FIRST PLACE IN A GAME OF FORTNITE BATTLE ROYALE IS CALLED A _____ ?

- [ ] **A.** #1 Spot
- [ ] **B.** Ice Cream Sundae
- [ ] **C.** Victory Royale

6 WHICH OF THESE IS NOT A HARVESTABLE MATERIAL IN FORTNITE?

- [ ] **A.** Brick
- [ ] **B.** Plastic
- [ ] **C.** Metal

7 WHAT'S THE NAME OF THE POPULAR, BUT MYSTERIOUS, LIQUID CONSUMED TO GAIN A PROTECTIVE BLUE SHIELD?

- [ ] **A.** Blu Juice
- [ ] **B.** Slurp
- [ ] **C.** Storm Sauce

8 WHICH OUTFIT IS NOT A SPORTS-BASED OPTION IN FORTNITE?

- [ ] **A.** Double Dribble
- [ ] **B.** Alpine Ace
- [ ] **C.** Fourth Down

9 WHICH OF THESE SHOWS A PLAYER BUILDING?

A

B

C

D

10 IDENTIFY THE ALL TERRAIN KARTS.

☐ **A.**

☐ **B.**

☐ **C.**

11 WHICH WEAPON DEBUTED IN CHAPTER 2: SEASON 1?

☐ **A.** Electric Net
☐ **B.** Scuba Suit
☐ **C.** Harpoon Gun

12 WHAT IS THE FORTNITE PHRASE "MATS" AN ABBREVIATION OF?

☐ **A.** Materials
☐ **B.** Matter
☐ **C.** Master

13

THIS DETAIL IS TAKEN FROM WHICH OUTFIT?

☐ **A.** Hollowhead
☐ **B.** Cuddle Team Leader
☐ **C.** Rabbit Raider

14

HOW MANY PLAYERS CAN BE PART OF A DUO?

☐ **A.** 4
☐ **B.** 2
☐ **C.** 3

15

FINISH THE FORTNITE PHRASE: BACK _____

☐ **A.** Bling
☐ **B.** Pack
☐ **C.** Bag

16 **WHICH OF THE FOLLOWING HAS NEVER BEEN A LOCATION ON THE FORTNITE MAP?**

☐ **A.** Dirty Docks
☐ **B.** Polar Peaks
☐ **C.** Barren Beach

17 **WHAT COLOR ARE EPIC WEAPONS?**

☐ **A.** Yellow
☐ **B.** Blue
☐ **C.** Purple

18 **WHAT ITEM, WHEN THROWN, INSTANTLY CREATES A SMALL BUILDING STRUCTURE WITH TIRES AT THE BOTTOM?**

☐ **A.** Instabuild
☐ **B.** Port-A-Fort
☐ **C.** Port-A-Tower

19 **WHICH BUILDING MATERIAL HAS THE MOST HEALTH?**

☐ **A.** Metal
☐ **B.** Wood
☐ **C.** Brick

ANSWERS P. 138

20 CAN YOU NAME THE LOCATION BY STUDYING THIS PICTURE?

- [ ] **A.** Frenzy Farm
- [ ] **B.** Fatal Fields
- [ ] **C.** Lazy Lake

21 WHAT IS THE NAME OF THE POPULAR BANANA CHARACTER IN FORTNITE?

- [ ] **A.** Nanaman
- [ ] **B.** Timothy Peel
- [ ] **C.** Peely

22 WHICH OF THE FOLLOWING IS NOT A TYPE OF BUILDING YOU CAN CREATE?

- [ ] **A.** Table
- [ ] **B.** Stairs
- [ ] **C.** Wall

23 WHICH VEHICLE HAS NOT APPEARED IN FORTNITE?

- [ ] **A.** Planes
- [ ] **B.** Trains
- [ ] **C.** Motorboats

24 WHICH OF THE FOLLOWING HELPED CELEBRATE THE MONTH OF FEBRUARY 2020?

- [ ] **A.** Love & War
- [ ] **B.** Leap Week
- [ ] **C.** Groundhog Wars

ANSWERS P. 138

25 **HOW MANY PLAYERS ARE THERE IN A BATTLE ROYALE MATCH?**

- [ ] **A.** 25
- [ ] **B.** 1000
- [ ] **C.** 100

26 **WHICH GAME MODE ARRIVED FIRST IN FORTNITE?**

- [ ] **A.** Creative
- [ ] **B.** Save The World
- [ ] **C.** Battle Royale

27 **WHAT COLOR IS MOST COMMONLY ASSOCIATED WITH AMMO BOXES?**

- [ ] **A.** Green
- [ ] **B.** Red
- [ ] **C.** Blue

28 **PLAYERS BEGIN A BATTLE ROYALE BY...**

- [ ] **A.** Cleaning Boots
- [ ] **B.** Swimming Ashore
- [ ] **C.** Jumping From A Bus

29

WHICH OF THESE WEAPONS IS THE DRUM GUN?

☐ A.

☐ B.

☐ C.

☐ D.

COMMON

☐ **A.**   ☐ **B.**   ☐ **C.**

30   **WHICH OF THESE OUTFITS IS DJ BOP?**

31   **WHAT IS THE HALLOWEEN-THEMED EVENT THAT TRADITIONALLY TAKES PLACE DURING OCTOBER?**

☐ **A.** Spookynite
☐ **B.** Fritenite
☐ **C.** Fortnitemares

32 WHICH HIGH-SPEED TRAVERSAL VEHICLE ALLOWED PLAYERS TO PULL OFF TRICKS?

☐ **A.** Driftboard
☐ **B.** Choppa
☐ **C.** Lasersled

33 WHICH COLOR COORDINATES WITH UNCOMMON LOOT RARITY?

☐ **A.** Pink
☐ **B.** Green
☐ **C.** Black

34 PICK OUT THE MEDKIT FROM THESE CHOICES.

☐ **A.**   ☐ **B.**   ☐ **C.**

COMMON

35 **WHAT DOES POI MEAN?**

- ☐ **A.** Player Of Interest
- ☐ **B.** Point Of Interest
- ☐ **C.** Pick On Intentionally

36 **IN WHICH YEAR WAS FORTNITE BATTLE ROYALE RELEASED?**

- ☐ **A.** 2015
- ☐ **B.** 2017
- ☐ **C.** 2019

37 **WHAT CAN A PLAYER USE TO GATHER MATERIALS?**

- ☐ **A.** Collecting Tool
- ☐ **B.** Vacuum
- ☐ **C.** Harvesting Tool

38 **SOMEONE WHO BROADCASTS LIVE FORTNITE GAMEPLAY IS A CALLED A...**

- ☐ **A.** Stringer
- ☐ **B.** Streamer
- ☐ **C.** Engineer

THE DURRR BURGER OUTFIT IS ALL MIXED UP. STARTING AT THE TOP, WHAT ORDER SHOULD THE STRIPS BE IN?

▢▢▢▢▢▢▢▢

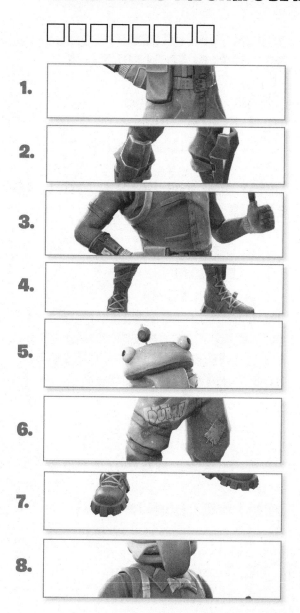

1.

2.

3.

4.

5.

6.

7.

8.

40 WHICH TYPE OF SPORTS ARENA HAS NOT APPEARED IN FORTNITE?

☐ **A.** Hockey Rink
☐ **B.** Soccer Field
☐ **C.** Basketball Court

41 WHAT WAS THE FIRST EMOTE IN FORTNITE BATTLE ROYALE?

☐ **A.** Dance Moves
☐ **B.** Default Dance
☐ **C.** Llama Drop

42 IN THE RIVERS AND OCEANS OF FORTNITE, WHICH ITEM CAN YOU NOT USE TO CATCH FISH?

☐ **A.** Fishing Rod
☐ **B.** Grappler Gun
☐ **C.** Harpoon Gun

43 WHAT ARE CRANKIN' 90S?

☐ **A.** Critical Hit
☐ **B.** Type Of Ammo
☐ **C.** Building Pattern

44 **WITH WEAPONS, WHAT DOES DPS MEAN?**

- ☐ **A.** Damage Per Second
- ☐ **B.** Detailed Precise Sight
- ☐ **C.** Detect Persons Soon

45 **WHICH OF THESE IS CLASSED AS AN EXPLOSIVE WEAPON?**

- ☐ **A.** Rocket Launcher
- ☐ **B.** Hunting Rifle
- ☐ **C.** Tactical Shotgun

46 **BONESY, CAMO, AND KYO ARE ALL TYPES OF WHAT?**

- ☐ **A.** Pet
- ☐ **B.** Glider
- ☐ **C.** Vehicle

47 **WHICH OF THESE ITEMS HELPS TO HIDE A PLAYER?**

- ☐ **A.** Emote
- ☐ **B.** Launch Pad
- ☐ **C.** Bush

ANSWERS P. 138

48 WHEN THROWN, WHAT CAN A BOOGIE BOMB MAKE THE OPPOSITION DO?

- ☐ **A.** Dance
- ☐ **B.** Freeze
- ☐ **C.** Become Invisible

49 IF SOMETHING IS REMOVED FROM FORTNITE, WHERE IS A POTENTIAL PLACE IT CAN BE KEPT?

- ☐ **A.** The Fridge
- ☐ **B.** The Vault
- ☐ **C.** The Trash

50 WHAT DOES PVP MEAN?

- ☐ **A.** Player Variance Perspective
- ☐ **B.** Player Versus Player
- ☐ **C.** Please View Properly

51 WHAT WAS THE FINAL SEASON IN CHAPTER 1?

- ☐ **A.** Season XX
- ☐ **B.** Season 6
- ☐ **C.** Season X

52 WHICH BUILDING MATERIAL COMPLETES THE FASTEST?

☐ **A.** Wood
☐ **B.** Metal
☐ **C.** Brick

53 WHAT DOES THIS SYMBOL REPRESENT?

☐ **A.** Damage
☐ **B.** Health
☐ **C.** Ammo

54 THE IN-GAME CURRENCY USED TO BUY COSMETICS IS CALLED...

☐ **A.** X-Bucks
☐ **B.** V-Bucks
☐ **C.** V-Coins

COMMON

55 THE NATURAL PHENOMENON THAT CAN CAUSE DAMAGE DURING A BATTLE ROYALE IS CALLED...

- ☐ **A.** The Storm
- ☐ **B.** The Hurricane
- ☐ **C.** The Wind

56 THIS FAMILIAR FACE IS A CHARACTER KNOWN AS WHAT?

☐ **A.** Jocky   ☐ **B.** Jimmy   ☐ **C.** Jonesy

57 WHEN ONE OF YOUR SQUADMATES IS ELIMINATED, THEY CAN RETURN TO THE GAME THROUGH A...

☐ **A.** Reboot Van
☐ **B.** Revive Station
☐ **C.** Doctor

58 WHAT IS THE SYSTEM THAT REWARDS PLAYERS FOR COMPLETING ACHIEVEMENTS?

☐ **A.** Allowance
☐ **B.** Battle Pass
☐ **C.** Big Battle

59 WHAT'S THE NAME OF THE PLACE WHERE COSMETICS CAN BE BOUGHT?

☐ **A.** Item Shop
☐ **B.** Item Store
☐ **C.** Item Market

60 WHAT MODE ALLOWS PLAYERS TO DESIGN, CREATE, AND EXPLORE THEIR OWN WORLD?

☐ **A.** Premium
☐ **B.** Imagination
☐ **C.** Creative

ANSWERS P. 139

61 IN THE 2018-19 SEASON, HOW MUCH DID EPIC GAMES PROVIDE IN ESPORT PRIZE POOLS?

- [ ] **A.** $10,000
- [ ] **B.** $100,000
- [ ] **C.** $100 million

62 AT THE BEGINNING OF WHICH SEASON DID THE MAP BECOME VERY FLOODED?

- [ ] **A.** Chapter 2: Season 1
- [ ] **B.** Chapter 2: Season 2
- [ ] **C.** Chapter 2: Season 3

63 CREATING PROTECTIVE WALLS VERY QUICKLY WHEN UNDER ATTACK IS COMMONLY REFERRED TO BY THE COMMUNITY AS...

- [ ] **A.** Fast Foraging
- [ ] **B.** Panic Building
- [ ] **C.** Snap Building

64 WHAT SET DO THESE AWESOME OUTFITS ALL BELONG TO?

- ☐ **A.** Skull Squad
- ☐ **B.** Bones Squad
- ☐ **C.** Scary Squad

ANSWERS P. 139

65 **WHICH OF THESE IS A MELEE WEAPON?**

- [ ] **A.** Infinity Blade
- [ ] **B.** Compact SMG
- [ ] **C.** Bolt-Action Sniper Rifle

66 **WHAT'S THE CLEVER ITEM THAT CAN HEAL MULTIPLE PLAYERS AT THE SAME TIME?**

- [ ] **A.** Cozy Campfire
- [ ] **B.** Blazin' Campfire
- [ ] **C.** Squad Campfire

67 **DURING WHICH SEASON DID THE BLACK HOLE APPEAR?**

- [ ] **A.** Season 9
- [ ] **B.** Chapter 2: Season 1
- [ ] **C.** Season X

68 **THE PERIOD IT TAKES FOR A WEAPON TO RELOAD IS CALLED...**

- [ ] **A.** Down Time
- [ ] **B.** Waiting Time
- [ ] **C.** Reload Time

69 **LAUNCHED IN CHAPTER 2: SEASON 3, WHICH SYSTEM ALLOWS PLAYERS TO CREATE THEIR OWN UMBRELLA?**

☐ **A.** Construct-A-Covering
☐ **B.** Build-A-Brella
☐ **C.** Um-Brella-Lievable

70 **HOW LONG IS A FORTNIGHT?**

☐ **A.** 2 Weeks
☐ **B.** 2 Years
☐ **C.** 2 Patches

FORTNITE
TRIVIA
UNCOMMON

71 **WHICH OF THE FOLLOWING IS A LOBBY TRACK?**

- ☐ **A.** "Battleblazers"
- ☐ **B.** "I'm A Cat"
- ☐ **C.** "Justified"

72 **WHICH SEA-DWELLING CREATURES WERE INTRODUCED WITH THE LAUNCH OF CHAPTER 2: SEASON 3?**

- ☐ **A.** Sharks
- ☐ **B.** Whales
- ☐ **C.** Dolphins

73 **WHAT WAS THE NAME OF THE TRAINING FIELD THAT FEATURED COMPETITIVE LEADERBOARDS?**

- ☐ **A.** The Arena
- ☐ **B.** The Challenge
- ☐ **C.** The Combine

74 **WHAT WAS THE FIRST STAR WARS OUTFIT TO APPEAR IN FORTNITE?**

- ☐ **A.** Stormtrooper
- ☐ **B.** Rey
- ☐ **C.** Kylo Ren

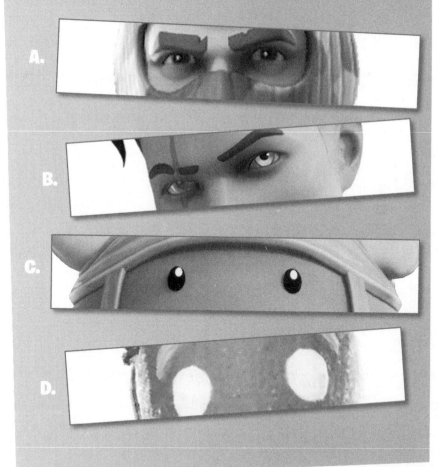

75 MATCH THE OUTFITS BELOW TO EACH OF THESE CLOSE-UP HEADSHOTS.

☐ 1. Guff
☐ 2. Havoc
☐ 3. Ginger Gunner
☐ 4. Midas

A.

B.

C.

D.

76 WHICH FAMOUS CHARACTER FROM ANOTHER GAME FRANCHISE APPEARED IN FORTNITE?

- ☐ **A.** Pac-Man
- ☐ **B.** Claptrap
- ☐ **C.** Q*bert

77 FORTNITE'S MOBILE APP IS ALSO KNOWN AS...?

- ☐ **A.** PartyUp
- ☐ **B.** FortFriends
- ☐ **C.** Party Hub

78 WHICH IS NOT A CORE GAME MODE OF FORTNITE?

- ☐ **A.** Duos
- ☐ **B.** Team Rumble
- ☐ **C.** Payload

79 WHO WAS VICTORIOUS IN THE FINAL SHOWDOWN?

- ☐ **A.** Robot
- ☐ **B.** Monster
- ☐ **C.** Mega Peely

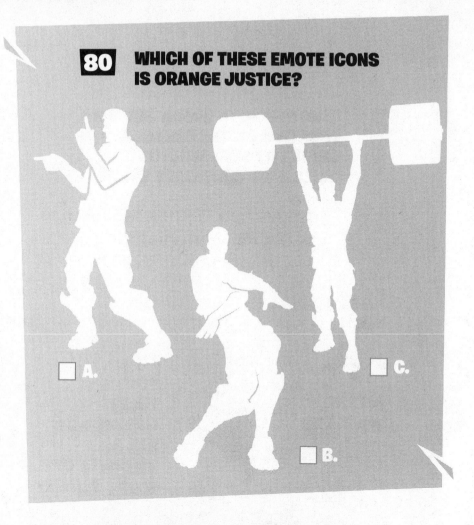

80 WHICH OF THESE EMOTE ICONS IS ORANGE JUSTICE?

☐ A.

☐ B.

☐ C.

81 WHAT SET WAS INCLUDED WITH THE XBOX ONE'S FORTNITE BATTLE ROYALE BUNDLE?

☐ **A.** Atomic Purple
☐ **B.** Vertex
☐ **C.** Purplex

82 "THE BLOCK," A BLANK SQUARE LOCATION ON THE FORTNITE CHAPTER 1 MAP, WOULD REGULARLY SHOWCASE WHAT?

- ☐ **A.** Live Epic Games HQ Footage
- ☐ **B.** Match Leaderboards
- ☐ **C.** Community-Made POI

83

THESE CHARACTERS ARE ALL VARIANTS OF WHICH OUTFIT?

- ☐ **A.** Wild Card
- ☐ **B.** 8-Ball vs Scratch
- ☐ **C.** Aquaman

84 WHO HAS AN ALTERNATE NAME OF "GOLDEN SKELETON"?

- ☐ **A.** Oro
- ☐ **B.** Goldnose
- ☐ **C.** Hazard Agent

85 WHAT CHARACTER PRESENTED FORTNITE FISHING FRENZY?

- ☐ **A.** Willy Water
- ☐ **B.** Fishstick
- ☐ **C.** Triggerfish

86 WHICH OF THESE MOBILITY ITEMS CAN PLAYERS USE BUT STILL TAKE FALL DAMAGE FROM?

- ☐ **A.** Impulse Grenade
- ☐ **B.** Shockwave Grenade
- ☐ **C.** Bouncer

87 WHICH OF THESE ITEMS TAKES UP TWO INVENTORY SLOTS?

- ☐ **A.** Rocket Launcher
- ☐ **B.** Bandage Bazooka
- ☐ **C.** Heavy Sniper

88 YOU ACCUMULATE _____ IN ARENA MODE WHEN GETTING ELIMINATIONS OR PLACING WELL.

- [ ] **A.** Rank
- [ ] **B.** Hype
- [ ] **C.** Score

89 WHICH OF THESE IS NOT A MATERIAL YOU CAN USE FOR BUILDING WITH?

- [ ] **A.** Plastic
- [ ] **B.** Wood
- [ ] **C.** Metal

90 WHAT TYPE OF AMMO DOES THE REVOLVER USE?

- [ ] **A.** Medium
- [ ] **B.** Light
- [ ] **C.** Heavy

91 WHO DEFENDS THE AGENCY?

- [ ] **A.** Bullies
- [ ] **B.** Henchmen
- [ ] **C.** Bouncers

92 WHICH OF THESE WEAPONS HAS NEVER APPEARED IN FORTNITE?

- ☐ **A.** Hand Cannon
- ☐ **B.** Heat-Seeking Missile
- ☐ **C.** Guided Missile

93 WHICH HEALING ITEM WILL RESTORE A PLAYER TO 100 HEALTH AND 100 SHIELD?

- ☐ **A.** Medkit
- ☐ **B.** Slurp Juice
- ☐ **C.** Chug Jug

94 WHAT WAS THE FIRST VEHICLE INTRODUCED INTO FORTNITE BATTLE ROYALE?

- ☐ **A.** Shopping Cart
- ☐ **B.** Quadcrasher
- ☐ **C.** Driftboard

95 WHAT PACK INCLUDES FROZEN RANGER?

- ☐ **A.** Ice Brigade
- ☐ **B.** Frozen Legends
- ☐ **C.** Winterfest Friends

96 **WHICH WAS THE FIRST VEHICLE WITH SUSTAINABLE FLIGHT?**

- [ ] **A.** Choppa
- [ ] **B.** X-4 Stormwing
- [ ] **C.** Motorboat

97 **WHEN WAS SWIMMING INTRODUCED?**

- [ ] **A.** Chapter 2: Season 1
- [ ] **B.** Chapter 2: Season 2
- [ ] **C.** Season X

98 **WHICH WEAPON HAS THE ABILITY TO MOVE A PLAYER'S POSITION WHEN SHOOTING?**

- [ ] **A.** Pump Shotgun
- [ ] **B.** Flint-Knock Pistol
- [ ] **C.** QuadLauncher

99 **WHO PERFORMED IN FORTNITE IN 2019?**

- [ ] **A.** Marshmello
- [ ] **B.** Travis Scott
- [ ] **C.** Diplo

100 WHICH ONE OF THESE HEALING ITEMS GIVES YOU 10 HEALTH WHEN CONSUMED?

☐ **A.** Pepper
☐ **B.** Banana
☐ **C.** Mushroom
☐ **D.** Slurpshroom
☐ **E.** Apple
☐ **F.** Coconut

101 WHICH OF THESE ITEMS IS ALSO PART OF THE BRUTE FORCE SET, ALONG WITH THE BRUTUS OUTFIT?

☐ **A.** Party Crashers
☐ **B.** Oozie
☐ **C.** Fusion Coil
☐ **D.** Hench Hauler

A.

B.

C.

D.

ANSWERS P. 139

102 WHICH OF THESE IS NOT AN LTM?

☐ **A.** Bounty
☐ **B.** Air Royale
☐ **C.** Slam Dunk

103 HOW MANY DEFAULT OUTFITS ARE THERE WHEN YOU START THE GAME?

☐ **A.** 4
☐ **B.** 6
☐ **C.** 8

104 WHAT WAS THE SLOGAN FOR CHAPTER 2: SEASON 3?

☐ **A.** Jump In
☐ **B.** Splash Down
☐ **C.** Swim To Win

105 WHICH OF THESE WAS ON THE MAP IN CHAPTER 2: SEASON 3?

☐ **A.** The Fortilla
☐ **B.** Snobby Shores
☐ **C.** Paradise Palms

106 **WHICH OF THESE IS A TAB IN FORTNITE CREATIVE?**

- ☐ **A.** Presentation
- ☐ **B.** Prefabs
- ☐ **C.** Prebuilds

107 **IDENTIFY THE GENUINE FORTNITE ESPORT EVENT...**

- ☐ **A.** Wicked Winter Series
- ☐ **B.** Shock Spring Series
- ☐ **C.** Summer Skirmish Series

108 **ONE OF THESE WRAPS IS PART OF THE SWOLE CAT SET. WHICH IS IT?**

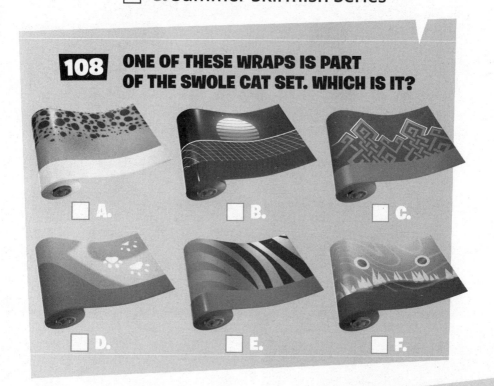

☐ **A.** ☐ **B.** ☐ **C.**

☐ **D.** ☐ **E.** ☐ **F.**

109 WHICH ONE OF THESE IMAGES IS FROM SEASON X?

A.

B.

C.

48

110 WHICH OF THESE POIS WAS NOT IN CHAPTER 1?

☐ **A.** Retail Row
☐ **B.** Craggy Cliffs
☐ **C.** Pleasant Park

111 WHICH OF THESE MODES IS INCLUDED IN SPY GAMES?

☐ **A.** Operation: Dumbo Drop
☐ **B.** Operation: Knockout
☐ **C.** Operation: Ridiculous

112 IN WHICH YEAR WAS FORTNITE BATTLE ROYALE AVAILABLE ON NINTENDO SWITCH?

☐ **A.** 2017
☐ **B.** 2018
☐ **C.** 2020

113 WHAT'S DESCRIBED AS A CELEBRATION OF FORTNITE "GAMING, MUSIC, FILM, AND FASHION"?

☐ **A.** Vision Series
☐ **B.** Hero Series
☐ **C.** Icon Series

114 WHICH OF THESE WAS A LIVE EVENT IN CHAPTER 2: SEASON 2?

- ☐ **A.** The Diner
- ☐ **B.** The Details
- ☐ **C.** The Device

115 WHICH OF THESE IS CONNECTED TO PROGRESSING AND LEVELING UP?

- ☐ **A.** Health
- ☐ **B.** XP
- ☐ **C.** Locker

116 THE TWO-PERSON ROBOT VEHICLE _____, INTRODUCED IN SEASON X, ALLOWED PLAYERS TO JUMP, BOOST, AND SHOOT ROCKETS.

- ☐ **A.** B.R.U.T.E.
- ☐ **B.** Mecha-Jonesy
- ☐ **C.** F0RT-3000

117 WHICH ONE IS NOT A VERSION OF PEELY?

- ☐ **A.** Prince Peely
- ☐ **B.** P-1000
- ☐ **C.** Agent Peely

118 WHAT IS THE NAME OF THE GIANT, DISRUPTIVE PURPLE CUBE IN FORTNITE CHAPTER 1?

☐ **A.** Cubey
☐ **B.** Kevin
☐ **C.** Frank

119 WHICH CONSUMABLE-MADE ITEMS FALL FROM THE SKY, BREAKING BUILDS AND DOING DAMAGE ON THEIR WAY TO THE GROUND?

☐ **A.** Storm Flip
☐ **B.** Rift-To-Go
☐ **C.** Junk Rift

120 WHERE WAS THE 2019 FORTNITE WORLD CUP HELD?

☐ **A.** Yankee Stadium
☐ **B.** Citi Field
☐ **C.** Arthur Ashe Stadium

121 IN WHICH SEASON WAS THE LAUNCH PAD INTRODUCED?

☐ **A.** Season 4
☐ **B.** Season 1
☐ **C.** Season 6

122 IN WINTERFEST, WHERE DID YOU OPEN CHRISTMAS PRESENTS?

- [ ] **A.** The Lobby
- [ ] **B.** The Lodge
- [ ] **C.** The Llama Den

123 HOW MANY SEASONS DID FORTNITE HAVE BEFORE CHAPTER 2?

- [ ] **A.** 10
- [ ] **B.** 1
- [ ] **C.** 100

124 WHICH OF THESE POIS WAS ON THE ISLAND IN SEASON 1?

- [ ] **A.** Lazy Lagoon
- [ ] **B.** Anarchy Acres
- [ ] **C.** Misty Meadows

125 WHICH ONE OF THESE IS NOT A TEAM LEADER?

- [ ] **A.** Rainbow
- [ ] **B.** P.A.N.D.A.
- [ ] **C.** Cuddle

126 WHICH ONE OF THESE OUTFITS IS NOT PART OF THE SPACE EXPLORERS SET?

☐ A.   ☐ B.   ☐ C.

☐ D.   ☐ E.   ☐ F.

127 IDENTIFY THE SLURPFISH HEALING ITEM FROM THESE SILHOUETTED SHAPES.

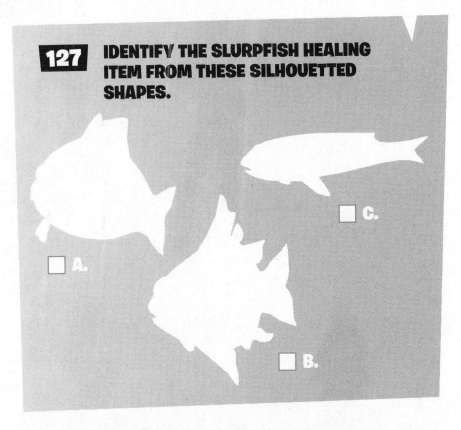

☐ **A.**

☐ **C.**

☐ **B.**

128 WHAT PART OF THE BATTLE ROYALE EXPERIENCE IS ALL ABOUT "HANGING OUT AND HAVING FUN"?

☐ **A.** Champion Series
☐ **B.** Support-A-Creator
☐ **C.** Party Royale

129 WHERE ON THE ISLAND WOULD YOU FIND CATTY CORNER?

- ☐ **A.** Southeast Corner
- ☐ **B.** Southwest Corner
- ☐ **C.** Northwest Corner

130 WHICH CHARACTER DOES THIS FLIPPER FOOT BELONG TO?

- ☐ **A.** Chomp Sr.
- ☐ **B.** Doublecross
- ☐ **C.** Alpine Ace

131 IN MAY 2020, EPIC GAMES ANNOUNCED THAT FORTNITE HAD REACHED WHAT MILESTONE?

☐ **A.** Over 100 Million Registered Players

☐ **B.** Over 350 Million Registered Players

☐ **C.** Over 1 Billion Registered Players

132 WHICH OUTFIT COMBINES STYLES FROM TOMATOHEAD, BEEF BOSS, REX, DRIFT, AND CUDDLE TEAM LEADER?

☐ **A.** Raven

☐ **B.** Beastmode

☐ **C.** Mecha Team Leader

133 IN WHICH SEASON DID EPIC GAMES REVEAL THE SPRAY ITEM?

☐ **A.** Chapter 2: Season 1

☐ **B.** Season 1

☐ **C.** Season 4

134 **NAME THE LTM WHICH FIRST RAN IN JUNE AND JULY 2019.**

- ☐ **A.** 14 Days Of Summer
- ☐ **B.** Hundred Hot Days
- ☐ **C.** Sun Special

135 **CABLE, DOMINO, AND PSYLOCKE ARE ALL PART OF WHAT SET?**

- ☐ **A.** A-Force
- ☐ **B.** X-Force
- ☐ **C.** Fierce Force

136 **WHICH COOL FEATURE DOES RISKY REELS HAVE?**

- ☐ **A.** Teleport Station
- ☐ **B.** Swimming Pool
- ☐ **C.** Drive-In Theater

137 **IN WHICH YEAR DID FORTNITE BATTLE ROYALE COME TO PHONES AND TABLETS?**

- ☐ **A.** 2017
- ☐ **B.** 2018
- ☐ **C.** 2021

138 WHICH OF THESE ARE REAL TYPES OF CODES YOU CAN DISCOVER AND ENTER IN FORTNITE?

- ☐ **A.** Island Codes
- ☐ **B.** Secret Codes
- ☐ **C.** Dress Codes

139 WHAT ADDITIONAL STYLES ARE THERE FOR THE SKYE OUTFIT, SHOWN OPPOSITE?

- ☐ **A.** Ghost, Shadow, And Golden Agent
- ☐ **B.** Bronze, Silver, And Gold
- ☐ **C.** Blue, Yellow, And Pink

140 WHICH OF THESE IS A SPY GAMES MODE?

- ☐ **A.** Operation: Ouch
- ☐ **B.** Operation: Infiltration
- ☐ **C.** Operation: Inspection

FORTNITE
TRIVIA

RARE

141 **WHAT IS THE TIER 38 BATTLE PASS OUTFIT IN CHAPTER 2: SEASON 4?**

- ☐ **A.** Groot
- ☐ **B.** Thor
- ☐ **C.** Doctor Doom

142 **WHAT REAL-TIME EVENT TOOK PLACE IN SEASON 4?**

- ☐ **A.** End Of The World
- ☐ **B.** Rocket Launch
- ☐ **C.** Giant Nuke

143 **WHERE DID MEOWSCLES FIRST APPEAR?**

- ☐ **A.** On The Computer
- ☐ **B.** In The Computer
- ☐ **C.** On A Yacht

144 **WHAT IS THE NAME OF SKYE'S RIDEABLE COMPANION?**

- ☐ **A.** Jolly
- ☐ **B.** Rollie
- ☐ **C.** Ollie

145 WHAT OUTFIT OFFERS THE MOST CUSTOMIZATION?

- [ ] **A.** Jonesy
- [ ] **B.** Peely
- [ ] **C.** Maya

146 WHAT'S THE NAME OF THE BACK BLING THAT GOES WITH THE HEADLOCK OUTFIT?

- [ ] **A.** Snappy
- [ ] **B.** Trappy
- [ ] **C.** Zappy

147 WHAT WAS THE FIRST RIDEABLE VEHICLE?

- [ ] **A.** B.R.U.T.E.
- [ ] **B.** Shopping Cart
- [ ] **C.** Golf Cart

148 WHEN DID THE RAISE THE CUP TOURNAMENT FIRST APPEAR?

- [ ] **A.** Chapter X
- [ ] **B.** Chapter 2: Season 1
- [ ] **C.** Chapter 2: Season 3

149 WHICH OF THESE HAS A DPS OF 200 OR MORE?

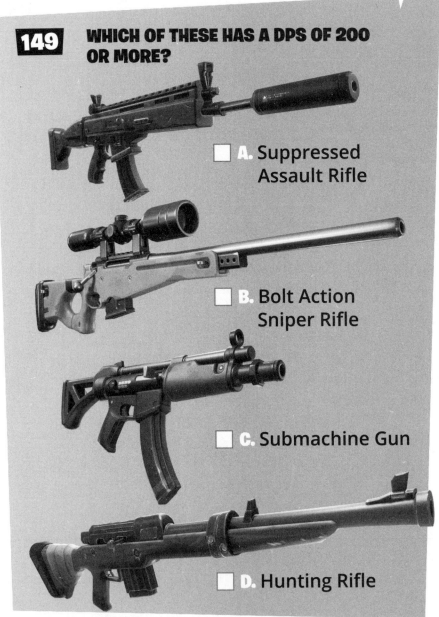

A. Suppressed Assault Rifle

B. Bolt Action Sniper Rifle

C. Submachine Gun

D. Hunting Rifle

150 IN 2019, WHAT AWARD DID FORTNITE WIN AT THE GAME AWARDS?

- [ ] **A.** Best Ongoing Game
- [ ] **B.** Best Island
- [ ] **C.** Best Battle

151 WHAT WAS THE NAME OF A CONTEST THAT ALLOWED PLAYERS TO CREATE A NEW EMOTE DANCE?

- [ ] **A.** EmoFest
- [ ] **B.** Groovathon
- [ ] **C.** Emote Royale

152 IN SEASON 9, MEGA MALL REPLACED WHICH LOCATION?

- [ ] **A.** Sweaty Sands
- [ ] **B.** Retail Row
- [ ] **C.** Slurpy Swamp

153 WHICH OF THESE LANDMARKS IS FOUND NEAR SLURPY SWAMP AND WEEPING WOODS?

- [ ] **A.** Logjam Woodworks
- [ ] **B.** Hayman
- [ ] **C.** Coral Cove

RARE

154 WHICH OF THESE LOCATIONS SHOWS THE EXPLODED OIL RIG?

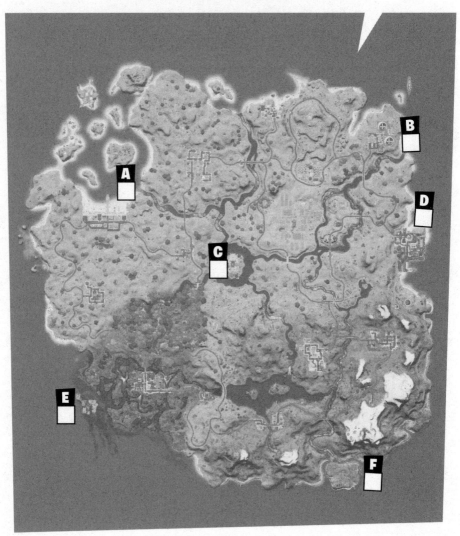

155 DURING WHICH SEASON WAS THE FORTNITE WORLD CUP HELD?

- [ ] **A.** Season 9
- [ ] **B.** Season X
- [ ] **C.** Chapter 2: Season 1

156 BOUNCING OFF ONE OF THESE IN SOLO, DUO, OR SQUAD MODE ALLOWS YOU TO REDEPLOY YOUR GLIDER.

- [ ] **A.** Bounce Pad
- [ ] **B.** Launch Pad
- [ ] **C.** Crash Pad

157 WHAT IS THE HEALTH OF THE MOTORBOAT?

- [ ] **A.** 600
- [ ] **B.** 1000
- [ ] **C.** 800

158 WHICH OF THESE IS NOT A BATTLE ROYALE EMOTE?

- [ ] **A.** Air Horn
- [ ] **B.** Jazz Hands
- [ ] **C.** Couch Slide

159 DRIVABLE CARS ARRIVED IN WHAT FORTNITE UPDATE?

- ☐ **A.** Joy Ride
- ☐ **B.** Top Speed
- ☐ **C.** Drive Time

160 WHICH SET ARE THESE TWO AWESOME OUTFITS FROM?

- ☐ **A.** Ice Kingdom
- ☐ **B.** Tech Ops
- ☐ **C.** Outbreak

161 WHICH OF THESE IS THE GRAPPLER?

☐ C.

☐ A.

☐ B.

162 WHERE IS THE EPIC GAMES HQ LOCATED?

☐ **A.** New York
☐ **B.** California
☐ **C.** North Carolina

163 WHICH OUTFIT, RELEASED IN 2020, HAS A TARGET ON THE CHEST AND BACK?

☐ **A.** Hit Man
☐ **B.** Contract Giller
☐ **C.** Fusion

164 WHICH OF THE FOLLOWING IS ASSOCIATED WITH BOTH AN OUTFIT SET AND A LTM?

- [ ] **A.** Arachnid
- [ ] **B.** Bigfoot
- [ ] **C.** Getaway

165 WHAT'S THE SYSTEM WHERE FANS CAN SUPPORT THEIR FAVORITE PLAYERS?

- [ ] **A.** Support-A-Creator
- [ ] **B.** Support-A-Pro
- [ ] **C.** Help-A-Friend

166 IN HONOR OF MARVEL'S DEADPOOL, WHAT PAIR OF OUTFITS WERE RELEASED IN 2020?

- [ ] **A.** Dark Red Knightpool And Dark Rexpool
- [ ] **B.** Copper Wasppool And Crypticpool
- [ ] **C.** Cuddlepool And Ravenpool

167 WHICH OF THE FOLLOWING IS A LOBBY TRACK?

☐ **A.** "Subterfuge"
☐ **B.** "Submarine"
☐ **C.** "Substitute"

168 IN WHICH SEASON WERE WRAPS INTRODUCED INTO BATTLE ROYALE?

☐ **A.** Season 5
☐ **B.** Season 7
☐ **C.** Season 9

169 WHEN DID THE SLURP LEGENDS PACK ARRIVE?

☐ **A.** Chapter 2: Season 2
☐ **B.** Chapter 2: Season 3
☐ **C.** Season X

170 HOW MANY PEOPLE CAN THE CHOPPA TRANSPORT?

☐ **A.** 3
☐ **B.** 4
☐ **C.** 5

RARE

171 **WHAT EVENT IN 2019 ALLOWED PLAYERS TO CHOOSE WEAPONS FROM THE VAULT?**

☐ **A.** The Upgrade Event
☐ **B.** The Unvaulting Event
☐ **C.** The Deep Dive Event

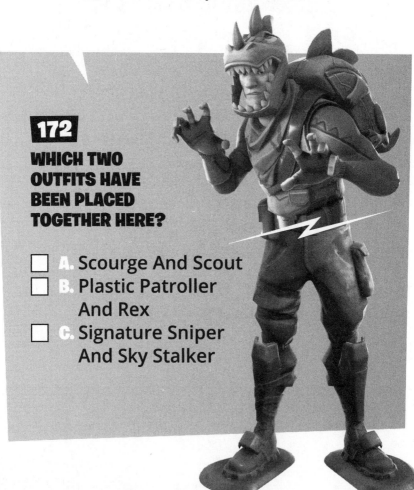

172

WHICH TWO OUTFITS HAVE BEEN PLACED TOGETHER HERE?

☐ **A.** Scourge And Scout
☐ **B.** Plastic Patroller And Rex
☐ **C.** Signature Sniper And Sky Stalker

173 **THIS IMAGE IS FROM AN EPIC GAMES VIDEO TRAILER FOR WHAT SEASON?**

☐ **A.** Chapter 2: Season 1
☐ **B.** Chapter 2: Season 2
☐ **C.** Chapter 2: Season 3

174 **WHAT TOOK PLACE ON FRIDAYS AND SATURDAYS IN MARCH AND APRIL 2020?**

☐ **A.** Hype Nite
☐ **B.** Hero Nite
☐ **C.** Nighty Nite

175 EPIC GAMES ORIGINATED IN WHICH US STATE?

- [ ] **A.** Texas
- [ ] **B.** Florida
- [ ] **C.** Maryland

176 FORTNITE'S SUMMER BLOCK PARTY TOOK PLACE AT THE FORUM LOCATION OF WHAT SPORTS TEAM?

- [ ] **A.** USC Trojans
- [ ] **B.** Los Angeles Lakers
- [ ] **C.** Los Angeles Dodgers

177 WHO OWNS THE PEOW PEOW RIFLE?

- [ ] **A.** Remedy vs Toxin
- [ ] **B.** Midas
- [ ] **C.** Meowscles

178 WHAT RARITY IS THE BRUTUS OUTFIT?

- [ ] **A.** Mythic
- [ ] **B.** Epic
- [ ] **C.** Legendary

179 DURING THE FORTNITE X BATMAN EVENT, WHICH RIFT ZONE WAS TRANSFORMED INTO GOTHAM CITY?

- ☐ **A.** Tilted Towers
- ☐ **B.** Greasy Groves
- ☐ **C.** Sweaty Sands

180 WHICH OF THESE WAS NOT A FIRST-WAVE NERF WEAPON?

- ☐ **A.** MG-L Scoped Automatic
- ☐ **B.** SP-L Nerf Elite Dart Blaster
- ☐ **C.** SP-L Elite Dart Blaster

181 WHAT ITEM APPEARED IN CHAPTER 2: SEASON 1 AND COULD CAUSE 20 DAMAGE?

- ☐ **A.** Fishing Rod
- ☐ **B.** Rusty Can
- ☐ **C.** Firefly Jar

182 WHICH BATMAN VARIANT HAS NOT APPEARED IN FORTNITE?

- ☐ **A.** Caped Crusader
- ☐ **B.** Batman Beyond
- ☐ **C.** Dark Knight

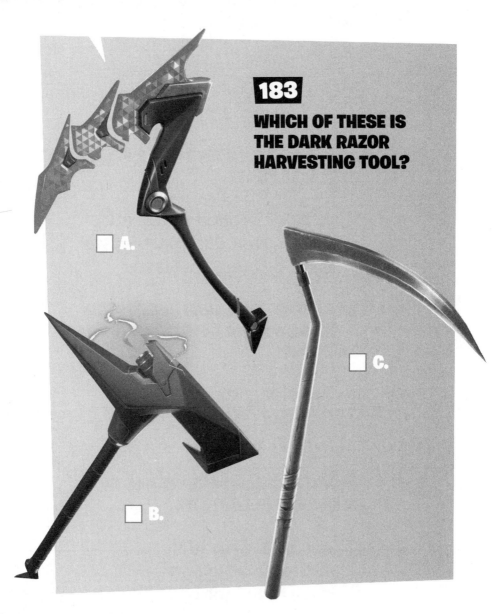

183

WHICH OF THESE IS THE DARK RAZOR HARVESTING TOOL?

☐ **A.**

☐ **B.**

☐ **C.**

184 BY JULY 2020, HOW MANY FORTNITE FOLLOWERS WERE THERE ON TWITCH?

- ☐ **A.** 6 Million
- ☐ **B.** 60 Million
- ☐ **C.** 600 Million

185 HOW MANY PLAYERS DO YOU NEED TO JOIN YOUR PARTY TO UNLOCK ACCESS TO THE "DRAGON SQUAD" IN SQUAD FORMATION?

- ☐ **A.** 13
- ☐ **B.** 3
- ☐ **C.** 5

186 WHICH OF THESE WAS NOT A REAL LTM IN BATTLE ROYALE?

- ☐ **A.** Fighting 50s
- ☐ **B.** Soaring 50s
- ☐ **C.** 50 vs 50

187 WHAT REGULARLY OVERHEATS IF FIRED TOO OFTEN?

- ☐ **A.** Compact SMG
- ☐ **B.** Burst Assault Rifle
- ☐ **C.** Mounted Turret

ANSWERS P. 141

188 WHICH OF THE FOLLOWING IS NOT A REAL FORAGED ITEM IN BATTLE ROYALE?

- ☐ **A.** Corn
- ☐ **B.** Cabbage
- ☐ **C.** Onion

189 WHAT SPECIAL ITEM ALLOWED PLAYERS TO BE INVISIBLE TO THE ENEMY?

- ☐ **A.** Shadow Stones
- ☐ **B.** Shadow Shields
- ☐ **C.** Shadow Trail

190 IN SEASON 9, WHAT DID TILTED TOWERS BECOME?

- ☐ **A.** Neo Tilted
- ☐ **B.** Never Tilted
- ☐ **C.** Totally Tilted

191 WHICH OF THESE IS FURTHER NORTH?

- ☐ **A.** Retail Row
- ☐ **B.** Lazy Lake
- ☐ **C.** Slurpy Swamp

192 WHICH OF THESE IS A STICKY EXPLOSIVE WEAPON?

- [ ] **A.** Clinger
- [ ] **B.** Clasper
- [ ] **C.** Gripper

193 WHAT ARE THE COORDINATES FOR CRAGGY CLIFFS?

- [ ] **A.** C1
- [ ] **B.** E1
- [ ] **C.** G1

194

FIGURE OUT WHO THIS OUTFIT IS FROM THIS CLOSE-UP.

- [ ] **A.** Perfect Shadow
- [ ] **B.** Sentinel
- [ ] **C.** Spider Knight

195 WHAT WAS THE SLOGAN FOR SEASON 8?

- ☐ **A.** The Final Farewell
- ☐ **B.** Worlds Collide
- ☐ **C.** X Marks the Spot

196 RAPSCALLION AND SCOUNDREL ARE PART OF WHICH SET?

- ☐ **A.** Pastel Patrol
- ☐ **B.** Crims
- ☐ **C.** Jailbird

197 WHAT'S THE NAME OF THE HOT DOG–INSPIRED OUTFIT FROM CHAPTER 2: SEASON 1?

- ☐ **A.** The Brat
- ☐ **B.** The Dog
- ☐ **C.** The Mustard

198 GWINNY IS A PENGUIN-INSPIRED...

- ☐ **A.** Glider
- ☐ **B.** Back Bling
- ☐ **C.** Outfit

WHICH OF THESE IS FROM THE E.G.O. GROUP?

☐ **A.**

☐ **B.**

☐ **C.**

200 WHICH OF THESE IS A PLAYSTATION-ONLY FORTNITE COMPETITION?

- [ ] **A.** PlayStation+
- [ ] **B.** Celebration Cup
- [ ] **C.** PerfectPlay

201 "ATTACK. DEFEND. CONQUER." THIS IS HOW EPIC GAMES DESCRIBED WHICH LTM?

- [ ] **A.** Solid Gold
- [ ] **B.** Food Fight
- [ ] **C.** Search And Destroy

202 COMPLETE THIS OUTFIT'S NAME: CAMEO VS _____

- [ ] **A.** Chic
- [ ] **B.** Chick
- [ ] **C.** Camo

203 WHICH OF THESE OUTFITS HAS NEON SELECTABLE STYLES?

- [ ] **A.** Jellie
- [ ] **B.** Llion
- [ ] **C.** Midas

204 **WHAT WAS THE 2020 PIZZA AND ICE CREAM-THEMED BUNDLE CALLED?**

- ☐ **A.** Scoops & Slices
- ☐ **B.** Cheese & Vanilla
- ☐ **C.** Sweet Tasting

205 **RIPPLEY VS SLUDGE'S HARVESTING TOOL IS CALLED...**

- ☐ **A.** Sludgeslayer
- ☐ **B.** Sludgehammer
- ☐ **C.** Sludge-Budger

206 **WHAT EXCITING ITEM ARRIVED AT THE START OF CHAPTER 2: SEASON 2?**

- ☐ **A.** Field Hunter Crossbow
- ☐ **B.** X-4 Stormwing
- ☐ **C.** Weapon Upgrade Bench

207 **HOW LONG DOES A BOOGIE BOMB TAKE HOLD FOR?**

- ☐ **A.** 5 Seconds
- ☐ **B.** 10 Seconds
- ☐ **C.** 20 Seconds

208 IN THE PUMPKIN PATCH SET, WHAT'S THE FIRST NAME OF THE GOURDON OUTFIT, AS SEEN ON THE OPPOSITE PAGE?

☐ **A.** Jack
☐ **B.** Jim
☐ **C.** Gordon

209 WHICH OF THESE IS A WEAPON IN SAVE THE WORLD AND NOT BATTLE ROYALE?

☐ **A.** Dual Pistols
☐ **B.** Charge Shotgun
☐ **C.** Cocoa.45

210 WHAT IS STICKS?

☐ **A.** An Outfit
☐ **B.** A Restaurant
☐ **C.** A Type Of Ammunition

FORTNITE
TRIVIA
EPIC

211 **WHAT TYPE OF AMMO DOES THE DRUM GUN TAKE?**

- [ ] **A.** Heavy
- [ ] **B.** Medium
- [ ] **C.** Light

212 **WHICH POI HAS NOMS LOCATED IN IT?**

- [ ] **A.** Retail Row
- [ ] **B.** Pleasant Park
- [ ] **C.** Lonely Lodge

213 **FNCS STANDS FOR...**

- [ ] **A.** Fortnite Champion Series
- [ ] **B.** Friday Night Champion Series
- [ ] **C.** Fortnite Competitive Series

214 **WHICH OF THESE IS NOT A MAP IN THE SEARCH AND DESTROY LTM?**

- [ ] **A.** Cove
- [ ] **B.** Factory
- [ ] **C.** Office

215 WHICH OF THESE OUTFITS IS FADE?

☐ A.

☐ B.

☐ C.

EPIC

216 WHAT WAS THE FIRST LTM FEATURED IN FORTNITE THAT WAS MADE IN CREATIVE MODE?

- ☐ **A.** Zone Wars
- ☐ **B.** Beach Assault
- ☐ **C.** Downtown Drop

217 WHO WAS THE LEVEL 100 REWARD FOR THE SEASON 3 BATTLE PASS?

- ☐ **A.** Red Knight
- ☐ **B.** The Reaper
- ☐ **C.** Black Knight

218 TACO TIME WOULD SEND PLAYERS INTO A FRENZY AT WHAT LOCATION?

- ☐ **A.** Greasy Grove
- ☐ **B.** Tilted Towers
- ☐ **C.** Flopper Pond

219 WHO DOES THE FIRST RIDEABLE GLIDER BELONG TO?

- ☐ **A.** Jonesy
- ☐ **B.** Meowscles
- ☐ **C.** TNTina

220 USE THE CHOICES GIVEN TO NAME EACH OUTFIT, JUST FROM THESE CLOSE-UP HEADSHOTS.

- ☐ **1.** 8-Ball
- ☐ **2.** Stingray
- ☐ **3.** Triggerfish
- ☐ **4.** Jolly Jammer

A.

B.

C.

D.

EPIC

221 **WHAT WAS THE FIRST SIDEGRADED WEAPON?**

- [ ] **A.** Heavy Assault Rifle
- [ ] **B.** Double Pump Shotgun
- [ ] **C.** Scoped AR

222 **WHERE DID FORTNITE'S ANNOUNCEMENT TRAILER DEBUT?**

- [ ] **A.** VGAs
- [ ] **B.** PAX
- [ ] **C.** E3

223 **WHICH TYPE OF SMG DOES NOT HAVE AN EPIC OR LEGENDARY VERSION OF IT?**

- [ ] **A.** Compact
- [ ] **B.** Tactical
- [ ] **C.** Burst

224 **WHICH EMOTE WAS REMIXED AS A LOBBY TRACK AFTER PLAYERS VOTED ON TWITTER?**

- [ ] **A.** Poplock
- [ ] **B.** Savor The W
- [ ] **C.** Freestylin'

225 WHO IS THE BOLD WARRIOR OF MOISTY MIRE?

☐ **A.** Blue Squire
☐ **B.** Leviathan
☐ **C.** Fishstick

226 WHICH NFL TEAM RECEIVED AN UPDATED UNIFORM IN FORTNITE PRIOR TO THE 2019 SEASON?

☐ **A.** New York Giants
☐ **B.** New York Jets
☐ **C.** New Orleans Saints

227 WHAT WAS THE FORTNITE CHAPTER 1 ISLAND'S SHAPE BASED OFF OF?

☐ **A.** Andromeda Galaxy
☐ **B.** Bob
☐ **C.** The Milky Way

228 WHICH SEASON DID NOT HAVE A BATTLE PASS?

☐ **A.** Season 1
☐ **B.** Season 2
☐ **C.** Season X

229 **WHICH OF THESE BLURRY WEAPONS IS THE RAPID FIRE SMG?**

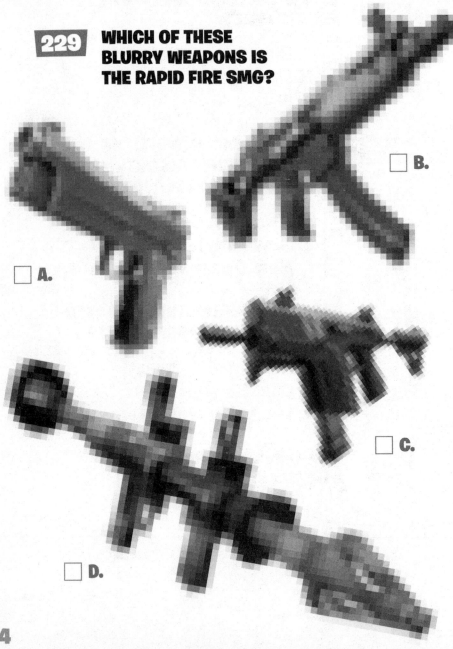

☐ **A.**

☐ **B.**

☐ **C.**

☐ **D.**

230 WHEN WAS THE SHAKEDOWN FEATURE INTRODUCED?

☐ **A.** Chapter 2: Season 3
☐ **B.** Chapter 2: Season 1
☐ **C.** Chapter 2: Season 2

231 WHICH OF THESE OUTFITS IS HEAVILY TATTOOED?

☐ **A.** Jules
☐ **B.** Sureshot
☐ **C.** Grill Sergeant

232 IN CREATIVE MODE, WHAT WAS THE GUNNER RENAMED AS?

☐ **A.** Sentry
☐ **B.** Turret
☐ **C.** Stevie

233 WHAT TYPE OF "FLIER" WAS EARNED FOR VICTORY IN CHAPTER 2: SEASON 3?

☐ **A.** Fearsome
☐ **B.** Fortilla
☐ **C.** Black

234 **WHO IS RELATED TO MEOWSCLES?**

☐ **A.** Kitten
☐ **B.** Kitty
☐ **C.** Kit

235 **THE 2020 EMOTE INSPIRED BY A DRAKE SONG IS CALLED...**

☐ **A.** The Toosie Emote
☐ **B.** The Toosie Slide Emote
☐ **C.** The Slide Emote

236 **WHICH OF THESE IS A REAL FORTNITE EVENT?**

☐ **A.** 13 Days Of Fortnite
☐ **B.** 14 Days Of Fortnite
☐ **C.** 15 Days Of Fortnite

237 **WHAT CHALLENGES WERE PART OF FORTNITE'S TEAM UP WITH MARVEL'S AVENGERS IN 2020?**

☐ **A.** H.A.R.M. Challenges
☐ **B.** H.E.R.O. Challenges
☐ **C.** H.E.A.T. Challenges

238 WHICH THREE OF THESE OUTFITS ARE NOT IN THE AEROSOL ASSASSINS SET?

A.

B.

C.

D.

E.

F.

239 **WHICH OF THESE CLOSE-UP PHOTOS SHOWS THE MOTORBOAT?**

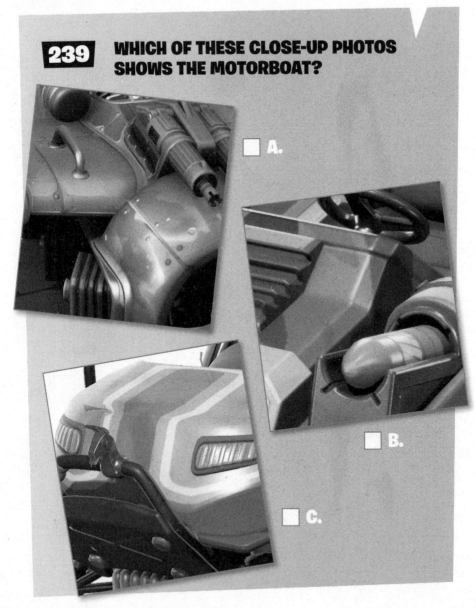

A.

B.

C.

240 WHICH POI WAS A NICE NEIGHBORHOOD ON THE WEST SIDE OF THE ISLAND IN CHAPTER 1, BEFORE IT WAS INVADED BY VIKINGS?

☐ **A.** Snobby Shores
☐ **B.** Greasy Grove
☐ **C.** Starry Suburbs

241 WHAT IS PANTHER'S PROWL?

☐ **A.** An Emote
☐ **B.** A Statue
☐ **C.** A Back Bling

242 PICK OUT THE MIDAS MEMORY WRAP, PART OF THE GOLDEN TOUCH SET, FROM THIS SELECTION...

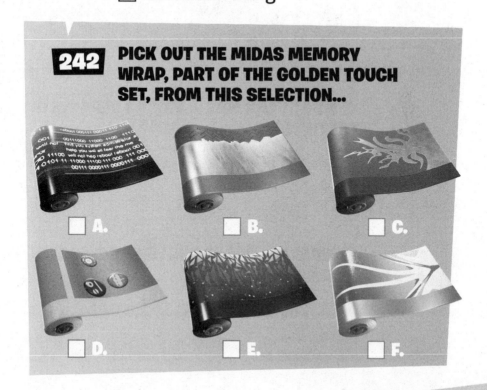

☐ **A.**   ☐ **B.**   ☐ **C.**

☐ **D.**   ☐ **E.**   ☐ **F.**

243 WHICH HAS NOT BEEN REPRESENTED WITH A VICTORY ROYALE UMBRELLA?

- ☐ **A.** Black Hole
- ☐ **B.** Spiderweb
- ☐ **C.** Hologram

244 WHICH SEASON TRAILER WAS REVEALED AT THE GAME AWARDS IN 2018?

- ☐ **A.** Season X
- ☐ **B.** Season 7
- ☐ **C.** Chapter 2: Season 2

245 IN WHAT YEAR WAS A MOBILE VERSION OF FORTNITE FIRST RELEASED?

- ☐ **A.** 2017
- ☐ **B.** 2018
- ☐ **C.** 2019

246 IN WHAT YEAR WAS FORTNITE OFFICIALLY ANNOUNCED?

- ☐ **A.** 2011
- ☐ **B.** 2012
- ☐ **C.** 2014

247 WHAT DATE WAS THE FIRST SEASON OF FORTNITE BATTLE ROYALE RELEASED?

☐ **A.** September 2017
☐ **B.** January 2018
☐ **C.** March 2018

248 WHAT'S THE SYSTEM THAT LETS STRUCTURES BUILD FASTER ONCE THE FIRST PIECE IS PLACED?

☐ **A.** Quick Build
☐ **B.** Fast Build
☐ **C.** Turbo Build

249 WHAT RARITY IS THE RIFT-TO-GO?

☐ **A.** Legendary
☐ **B.** Epic
☐ **C.** Mythic

250 IN CHAPTER 2: SEASON 2, WHAT WERE THE COORDINATES FOR THE SHARK POI?

☐ **A.** B1
☐ **B.** A1
☐ **C.** D1

251 **PROPANE TANKS WERE PART OF WHICH SEASON?**

☐ **A.** Chapter 2: Season 2
☐ **B.** Chapter 2: Season 3
☐ **C.** Chapter 2: Season 1

252 **WHAT WAS THE FIRST VEHICLE TO HAVE A BUILT-IN WEAPON?**

☐ **A.** Pirate Cannon
☐ **B.** X-4 Stormwing
☐ **C.** ATK

253 **WHICH OF THESE HATS IS PART OF THE BIRDIE OUTFIT?**

254 MARK WHERE HOLLY HEDGES IS, AFTER IT ARRIVED ON THE MAP IN CHAPTER 2: SEASON 1.

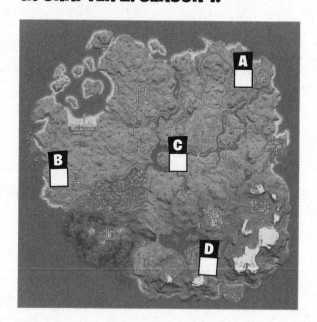

255 WHICH OF THESE IS A THROWN EXPLOSIVE ITEM?

- ☐ **A.** Proximity Bomb
- ☐ **B.** Proximity Mine
- ☐ **C.** Proximity Launcher

256 WHICH BATTLE PASS TRAILER BEGAN BY SAYING "WELCOME TO THE WAVES"?

- ☐ **A.** Chapter 2: Season 3
- ☐ **B.** Chapter 2: Season 1
- ☐ **C.** Season 7

257 INTRODUCED IN CHAPTER 2: SEASON 3, WHAT WEAPON CAN START FIRES?

☐ **A.** Fire Gun
☐ **B.** Flare Gun
☐ **C.** Flash Gun

258 WHICH OF THESE ITEMS WAS VAULTED IN PATCH 10.20?

☐ **A.** Small Shield Potion
☐ **B.** Hunting Rifle
☐ **C.** Storm Flip

259 WHICH OF THESE TRAPS IS IN SAVE THE WORLD AND NOT BATTLE ROYALE?

☐ **A.** Sound Wall
☐ **B.** Crash Pad
☐ **C.** Chiller

260 WHAT DID EPIC GAMES INTRODUCE IN THE SEASON 5 BATTLE PASS?

☐ **A.** Pets
☐ **B.** Toys
☐ **C.** Bananas

261 THESE ARE ALL VARIANTS OF WHICH GLIDER?

- [ ] **A.** Fuel
- [ ] **B.** Fusion Coil
- [ ] **C.** Fossil Flyer

262 WHAT CHALLENGES WERE PART OF THE SEASON 4 BATTLE PASS?

- [ ] **A.** Ragnarok Challenges
- [ ] **B.** Aquaman Challenges
- [ ] **C.** Omega Challenges

263 WHICH OF THESE IS A VARIANT OF THE SIONA OUTFIT?

- [ ] **A.** Spacewalk
- [ ] **B.** Nevada
- [ ] **C.** Crimson

264 **WHICH BATTLE PASS BEGAN ON MAY 1, 2018?**

☐ **A.** Season 3
☐ **B.** Season 4
☐ **C.** Season 5

265 **WHAT WAS ONLY AVAILABLE IN SEASON 1?**

☐ **A.** Weapons Shop
☐ **B.** Season Shop
☐ **C.** V-Bucks Shop

266 **WHAT WAS THE FOG OF WAR LTM PREVIOUSLY KNOWN AS?**

☐ **A.** Team Rumble
☐ **B.** Final Fight
☐ **C.** Sneaky Silencers

267 **WHAT WAS LAUNCHED IN APRIL 2020?**

☐ **A.** Fortnite Creator Contest
☐ **B.** Fortnite Spray Contest
☐ **C.** Fortnite Dance Contest

268 IN WHICH YEAR DID EPIC GAMES ENCOURAGE PLAYERS TO "UNLOCK YOUR TEAM OF DRIFTERS"?

- [ ] **A.** 2020
- [ ] **B.** 2019
- [ ] **C.** 2918

269 WITH THUMB AND LITTLE FINGER POINTING UP FROM A HAND, AND PALM TREES EITHER SIDE, THIS SYMBOL REPRESENTED...

- [ ] **A.** Summer Skirmish Series
- [ ] **B.** Fortnite Summer Splash
- [ ] **C.** Fortnite Summer Showdown

270 WHAT IS BOOTY BUOY?

- [ ] **A.** Glider
- [ ] **B.** Emote
- [ ] **C.** POI

271 WHAT'S THE NAME OF THE FIRST DRIVABLE PICKUP TRUCK?

- [ ] **A.** Islander Prevalent
- [ ] **B.** Whiplash
- [ ] **C.** Bear

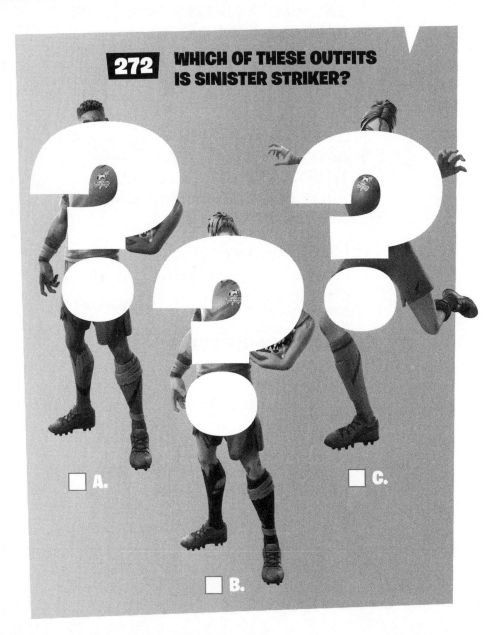

272 **WHICH OF THESE OUTFITS IS SINISTER STRIKER?**

☐ A.

☐ B.

☐ C.

273 COMPLETE THE REST OF THIS CHARACTER: BLOCKADE _____

- [ ] **A.** Runner
- [ ] **B.** Blast
- [ ] **C.** Storm

274 WHICH OUTFIT IS DESCRIBED AS "COZY COMBAT, FRESH TO YOUR DOOR"?

- [ ] **A.** Tomatohead
- [ ] **B.** PJ Pepperoni
- [ ] **C.** Onesie

275 WHICH WEAPON FIRST ARRIVED IN SEASON 7, DEALING 45 DAMAGE IN THE RARE VARIANT?

- [ ] **A.** Scoped Assault Rifle
- [ ] **B.** Infantry Rifle
- [ ] **C.** Combat Shotgun

276 WHICH DEVICE SHOT A BEAM OF ELECTRICITY INTO THE SKY?

- [ ] **A.** Bright Beacon
- [ ] **B.** Rift-To-Go
- [ ] **C.** Rift Beacon

277 **WHERE WOULD YOU FIND STARK ROBOTS?**

- ☐ **A.** Quinjet Patrol Sites
- ☐ **B.** Doom's Domain
- ☐ **C.** The Fortilla

278 **WHAT WERE BEING SEARCHED FOR IN THE ENDGAME LTM?**

- ☐ **A.** Infinity Stones
- ☐ **B.** Infinity Blades
- ☐ **C.** Mythic Chests

279 **WHAT WAS THE LTM WHERE ONLY THROWN OR TOSSED GRENADES AND EXPLOSIVES COULD BE USED?**

- ☐ **A.** ThrowThru
- ☐ **B.** Catch
- ☐ **C.** Watch Out

280 WHICH OF THESE OUTFITS IS TRENCH RAIDER?

☐ A.

☐ B.

☐ C.

ANSWERS P. 143

FORTNITE
TRIVIA
LEGENDARY

281 WHAT'S THE PLACE WHERE TOILETS ARE MADE IN BATTLE ROYALE?

- ☐ **A.** Flush Building
- ☐ **B.** Flush HQ
- ☐ **C.** Flush Factory

282 WHICH OF THESE WAS VAULTED IN CHAPTER 2: SEASON 1?

- ☐ **A.** Wall Dynamo
- ☐ **B.** Zapper Trap
- ☐ **C.** Ceiling Zapper

283 IN WHICH YEAR DID THE SOCCER STADIUM ARRIVE AND DISAPPEAR?

- ☐ **A.** 2018
- ☐ **B.** 2017
- ☐ **C.** 2019

284 WHAT WAS DESCRIBED AS A WIND TRANSPORTATION SYSTEM?

- ☐ **A.** Turbine Track
- ☐ **B.** Slipstream
- ☐ **C.** Wind Whisk

285 **WHICH TWO OF THESE OUTFITS GO TOGETHER?**

☐ A.   ☐ B.   ☐ C.

☐ D.   ☐ E.   ☐ F.

LEGENDARY

286 IN WHAT SEASON DID THE WIND TRANSPORTATION SYSTEM ARRIVE?

- ☐ **A.** Season 9
- ☐ **B.** Season X
- ☐ **C.** Chapter 2: Season 1

287 NEW TO CHAPTER 2: SEASON 4, WHAT FILLED A "COLLECTORS' EDITION" WITH ITS VARIED SIZES, COLORS, AND RATINGS?

- ☐ **A.** Outfits
- ☐ **B.** Vehicles
- ☐ **C.** Fish

288

WHAT'S THE NAME OF THIS EMOTICON?

- ☐ **A.** Fire Drop
- ☐ **B.** Flame Drop
- ☐ **C.** Hot Drop
- ☐ **D.** Blaze Drop

289

WHOSE EYE IS THIS?

- [ ] **A.** Cuddle Team Leader
- [ ] **B.** Quackling
- [ ] **C.** Airhead

290 HOW WAS ULTIMA KNIGHT OBTAINED IN SEASON X?

- [ ] **A.** Tier 100 Reward
- [ ] **B.** Tier 50 Reward
- [ ] **C.** Item Shop

291 WHAT IS AIRLIFT?

- [ ] **A.** LTM
- [ ] **B.** Outfit
- [ ] **C.** Glider

292 WHAT IS THE NAME OF THE MOVIE SCREEN LOCATED ON PARTY ROYALE'S ISLAND?

- ☐ **A.** Big Screen
- ☐ **B.** Movie Screen
- ☐ **C.** Film Screen

293 WHAT WERE THE COORDINATES FOR THE GROTTO?

- ☐ **A.** C6
- ☐ **B.** B5
- ☐ **C.** H5

294 WHICH CHARACTER WAS PART OF THE NINTENDO SWITCH BUNDLE?

- ☐ **A.** Double Helix
- ☐ **B.** Double Agent Hush
- ☐ **C.** Double Agent Wildcard

295 WHICH OF THESE IS NOT A REAL BATTLE ROYALE OUTFIT?

- ☐ **A.** Ex
- ☐ **B.** Extra
- ☐ **C.** Ether

296 WHAT COMPETITIVE FORTNITE EVENT WAS ANNOUNCED IN MARCH 2020?

- ☐ **A.** Hype Nite
- ☐ **B.** Hype Nite+
- ☐ **C.** Celebration Cup

297 WHICH WEAPON DO YOU SPAWN WITH AFTER BEING REBOOTED?

- ☐ **A.** Common AR
- ☐ **B.** Common Pistol
- ☐ **C.** Common SMG

298 WHAT WAS UNVAULTED IN THE SPY GAMES LTM?

- ☐ **A.** Bottle Rockets
- ☐ **B.** Shield Bubble
- ☐ **C.** Chiller Grenade

299 WHAT WAS THE ORIGINAL MAGAZINE SIZE FOR THE DRUM GUN?

- ☐ **A.** 50
- ☐ **B.** 40
- ☐ **C.** 30

300 WHAT WAS MADE AT THE BOX FACTORY?

- [ ] **A.** Creepin' Cardboard
- [ ] **B.** Camo Cardboard
- [ ] **C.** Ammo Box

301 WHICH OF THESE IS A FORTNITE ESPORT EVENT?

- [ ] **A.** FortStars
- [ ] **B.** FT Stars
- [ ] **C.** TFTW Stars

302 WHAT WAS THE LTM THAT SAW VANS FLOAT IN MIDAIR?

- [ ] **A.** High Jewels
- [ ] **B.** Getaway
- [ ] **C.** Quick Heist

303 WHICH WEAPON RELOADS TWO SHELLS AT A TIME?

- [ ] **A.** Hunting Rifle
- [ ] **B.** Pump Shotgun
- [ ] **C.** Combat Shotgun

304 WHICH OF THESE IS THE MAP FROM CHAPTER 2: SEASON 1?

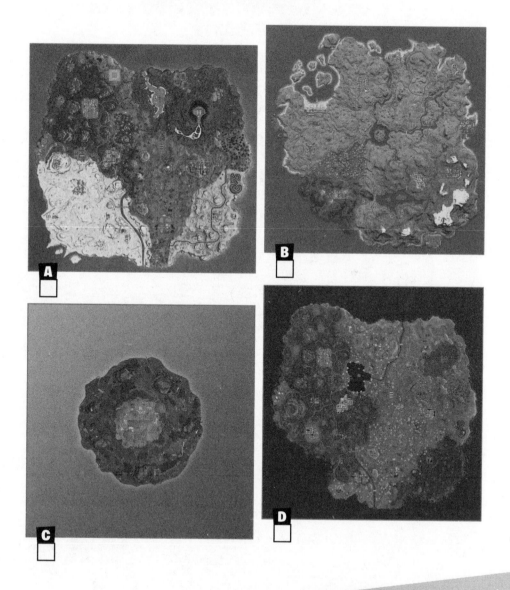

A

B

C

D

LEGENDARY

305 WHICH OF THESE BACK BLINGS HAS A DIAMOND VARIANT?

- ☐ **A.** Crystal Llama
- ☐ **B.** Eternal Shield
- ☐ **C.** Fallen Wings

306 WHAT HEALTH DID THE BALLER HAVE WHEN IT ARRIVED IN SEASON 8?

- ☐ **A.** 200
- ☐ **B.** 300
- ☐ **C.** 400

307 WHICH OF THESE OUTFITS IS SCUBA JONESY?

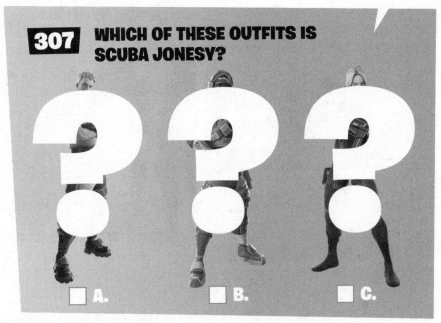

☐ **A.**   ☐ **B.**   ☐ **C.**

308 WHAT IS THIS CHAPTER 2: SEASON 3 LOADING SCREEN CALLED?

- [ ] **A.** SK8 Girl
- [ ] **B.** SK8-Bit
- [ ] **C.** SK8 Screen

309 WHICH EMOTE SEES YOU WAVE YOUR HAND IN THE AIR?

- [ ] **A.** Hello!
- [ ] **B.** Over Here!
- [ ] **C.** Taxi!

310 WHAT IS X?

- [ ] **A.** Back Bling
- [ ] **B.** Umbrella
- [ ] **C.** LTM

LEGENDARY

311 WHAT IS CAPTAIN AMERICA'S EMOTE CALLED?

- ☐ **A.** Grand Salute
- ☐ **B.** Shield Salute
- ☐ **C.** Cap's Salute

312 WHAT ARE "HIDE THE PAIN" AND "TOURIST TRAP"?

- ☐ **A.** POIs
- ☐ **B.** Back Blings
- ☐ **C.** Legacies

313 WHAT WAS THE MYTHIC CHUG JUG IN CHAPTER 2: SEASON 3 KNOWN AS?

- ☐ **A.** Infinite Chug Jug
- ☐ **B.** Ocean's Bottomless Chug Jug
- ☐ **C.** Rechargeable Chug Jug

314 WHICH DEV TEAM WORKED ON THE POPULAR PROP HUNT COMMUNITY MOD?

- ☐ **A.** NiteKite
- ☐ **B.** HighKite
- ☐ **C.** StrayKite

315 WHAT DID EPIC GAMES DESCRIBE AS "CRASHING DOWN ONTO THE ISLAND AND CHALLENGING YOUR SURVIVAL"?

☐ **A.** Marauders
☐ **B.** Henchmen
☐ **C.** Rifts

316 EPIC GAMES SAYS TO USE THIS ITEM TO "TURN UP THE HEAT ON YOUR OPPONENTS"...

☐ **A.** Firefly Jar
☐ **B.** Tactical Shotgun
☐ **C.** Flare Gun

317 IN EARLY 2020, WHAT SYSTEM DID EPIC GAMES MOVE FORTNITE TO?

☐ **A.** Unreal Engine's Monster Physics
☐ **B.** Unreal Engine's Chaos Physics
☐ **C.** Unreal Engine's Zero Physics

318 WHAT WAS THE LAUNCH DATE OF CHAPTER 2: SEASON 2?

☐ **A.** February 20, 2020
☐ **B.** March 1, 2020
☐ **C.** March 20, 2020

319 WHICH OF THESE IS AN OUTFIT UNLOCKED AT LEVEL 1 OF THE CHAPTER 2: SEASON 3 BATTLE PASS?

- [ ] **A.** Fade
- [ ] **B.** Shade
- [ ] **C.** Made

320 WHAT WAS FORTNITE'S FIRST NFL-THEMED EVENT CALLED?

- [ ] **A.** Fortnite X NFL
- [ ] **B.** Fortnite Teams NFL
- [ ] **C.** Fortnite Touch Down NFL

321 IN WHICH YEAR WAS THAT NFL EVENT?

- [ ] **A.** 2017
- [ ] **B.** 2018
- [ ] **C.** 2019

322 IN WHICH UPDATE DID BATTLE LAB APPEAR?

- [ ] **A.** 11.31
- [ ] **B.** 13.0
- [ ] **C.** 5.40

323 WHICH OF THESE OUTLINES IS OF THE SHADOWBIRD OUTFIT?

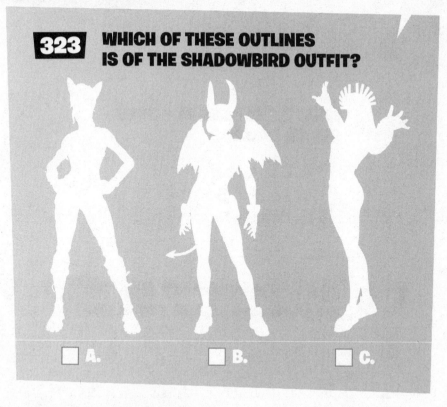

☐ **A.**   ☐ **B.**   ☐ **C.**

324 HOW MANY NUMBERS ARE IN AN ISLAND CODE?

☐ **A.** 8
☐ **B.** 10
☐ **C.** 12

325 WHAT CAME WITH THE MESSAGE "WARNING: MAY CAUSE COLD TOES"?

☐ **A.** Freezing Point Back Bling
☐ **B.** Chiller Grenade
☐ **C.** Ice Cream

326 WHAT'S THE BANANA ROYALE GLIDER CALLED?

- ☐ **A.** Banana Bomber
- ☐ **B.** Peely's Bomber
- ☐ **C.** Yellow Skin

327 CAN YOU IDENTIFY THE DUAL PISTOLS WEAPON, JUST FROM THESE SHAPES?

☐ **A.**

☐ **B.**

☐ **C.**

328

WHAT SET DOES THE ANTIDOTE BACK BLING BELONG TO?

- ☐ **A.** Bad Medicine
- ☐ **B.** Grim Medicine
- ☐ **C.** Team Toxic

329

WHICH OF THESE WAS NOT A PUNCH CARD?

- ☐ **A.** Weapon Whisperer
- ☐ **B.** Bullseye
- ☐ **C.** Boss Party

330

THE BABA YAGA OUTFIT HAS WHAT TIED AROUND HER WAIST?

- ☐ **A.** Toadstools
- ☐ **B.** Bottles Of Potions
- ☐ **C.** Chicken Legs

331 WHAT AMMO BOX DID THE BOOM BOW USE?

- [ ] **A.** Arrows
- [ ] **B.** Shotgun Shell
- [ ] **C.** Heavy Bullets

332 WHAT EVENT DID FORTNITE CELEBRATE IN APRIL 2020?

- [ ] **A.** Astroturf
- [ ] **B.** Astrospesh
- [ ] **C.** Astronomical

333 INSTANT-BUILD STRUCTURES IN CREATIVE ARE CALLED...

- [ ] **A.** Prefabs
- [ ] **B.** Prebuilds
- [ ] **C.** Snapbuilds

334 WHAT WEAPONS CAN BE USED IN THE FOG OF WAR LTM?

- [ ] **A.** Suppressed
- [ ] **B.** Uncommon
- [ ] **C.** Explosive

335 WHICH OF THESE IS NOT PART OF THE FEEDING FRENZY SET?

☐ **A.** Comfy Chomps
☐ **B.** Cozy Chomps
☐ **C.** Chomp Sr.

336 WHAT WAS THE SECOND VERSION OF THE SOLID GOLD LTM CALLED?

☐ **A.** Solid Gold: Reloaded
☐ **B.** Solid Gold V2
☐ **C.** Pure Solid Gold

337

WHICH TWO OUTFITS HAVE BEEN PUT TOGETHER HERE?

☐ **A.** Tailor And Warpaint
☐ **B.** Sureshot And Drift
☐ **C.** Hugo And Cloudbreaker

338 WHAT ITEM DID FORTNITE REVEAL IN ITS 4.20 CONTENT UPDATE?

- [ ] **A.** Skye's Grappler
- [ ] **B.** Shadow Bomb
- [ ] **C.** Jetpack

339 WHICH OF THESE IS AN ADJUSTMENT EPIC GAMES CAN MAKE TO FORTNITE GAMEPLAY?

- [ ] **A.** Hotfix
- [ ] **B.** Switchfix
- [ ] **C.** Flyfix

340 WHAT'S THE STRUCTURAL DAMAGE OF THE LEGENDARY QUAD LAUNCHER?

- [ ] **A.** 330
- [ ] **B.** 320
- [ ] **C.** 300

341 IN PATCH 11.30, WHAT FEATURE DID EPIC GAMES GIVE AN EARLY RELEASE TO?

- [ ] **A.** Carrying Knocked Squad Member
- [ ] **B.** Split Screen
- [ ] **C.** B.R.U.T.E. Vehicle

342 HOW MANY ROCKETS COULD THE PROXIMITY GRENADE LAUNCHER HOLD AT A TIME?

☐ **A.** 1
☐ **B.** 2
☐ **C.** 10

343 WHEN IT WAS FIRST RELEASED, WHAT DID THE CHUG SPLASH GRANT?

☐ **A.** 50 Shield To All Squad
☐ **B.** Full Health Or Shield
☐ **C.** 20 Health Or Shield

344 IT'S BEEN BLURRED, BUT WHICH GLIDER IS THIS?

☐ **A.** Retaliator
☐ **B.** Cyclone
☐ **C.** Stunt Cycle
☐ **D.** Y-Wing

LEGENDARY

345 IN WHICH MONTH DOES EPIC GAMES CELEBRATE FORTNITE'S BIRTHDAY?

- [ ] **A.** July
- [ ] **B.** June
- [ ] **C.** January

346 THE METEOR PROP IS A _____

- [ ] **A.** Gallery
- [ ] **B.** LTM
- [ ] **C.** Loading Screen

347

WHOSE HAND IS THIS?

- [ ] **A.** Bush Ranger
- [ ] **B.** Fishstick
- [ ] **C.** Bone Wasp

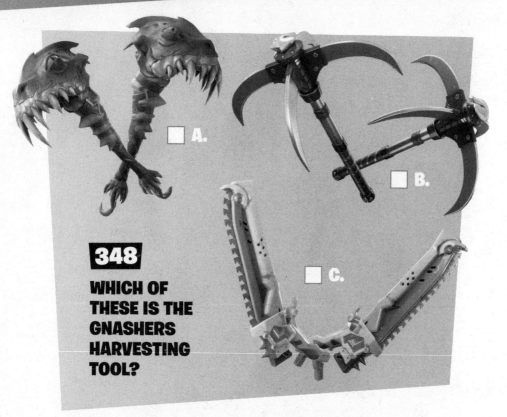

348

WHICH OF THESE IS THE GNASHERS HARVESTING TOOL?

☐ **A.**

☐ **B.**

☐ **C.**

349 **WHICH OF THESE OUTFITS DOES NOT HAVE A LLAMA-STYLE HEAD?**

☐ **A.** Lt. Evergreen
☐ **B.** Y0ND3R
☐ **C.** Bash

350 **WHO DOES EPIC GAMES CALL THE "QUEEN OF SUNSHINE"?**

☐ **A.** Brite Bomber
☐ **B.** Beach Bomber
☐ **C.** Sun Strider

FORTNITE TRIVIA
ANSWERS

COMMON

1.	B	19.	A	37.	C
2.	A	20.	A	38.	B
3.	A	21.	C	39.	5, 8, 3, 1, 6, 2, 4, 7
4.	C	22.	A		
5.	C	23.	B	40.	A
6.	B	24.	A	41.	A
7.	B	25.	C	42.	B
8.	A	26.	B	43.	C
9.	A	27.	A	44.	A
10.	C	28.	C	45.	A
11.	C	29.	C	46.	A
12.	A	30.	A	47.	C
13.	B	31.	C	48.	A
14.	B	32.	A	49.	B
15.	A	33.	B	50.	B
16.	B	34.	B	51.	C
17.	C	35.	B	52.	A
18.	B	36.	B	53.	C

54.	B	60.	C	66.	A
55.	A	61.	C	67.	C
56.	C	62.	C	68.	C
57.	A	63.	B	69.	B
58.	B	64.	A	70.	A
59.	A	65.	A		

UNCOMMON

71.	B	82.	C	94.	A
72.	A	83.	A	95.	B
73.	C	84.	A	96.	B
74.	A	85.	C	97.	A
75.	1:C, 2:A, 3:D, 4:B	86.	A	98.	B
		87.	B	99.	A
76.	B	88.	B	100.	D
77.	C	89.	A	101.	D
78.	C	90.	A	102.	C
79.	A	91.	B	103.	C
80.	B	92.	B	104.	B
81.	B	93.	C	105.	A

ANSWERS

106. B	**118.** B	**130.** A
107. C	**119.** C	**131.** B
108. D	**120.** C	**132.** C
109. B	**121.** B	**133.** C
110. B	**122.** B	**134.** A
111. B	**123.** A	**135.** B
112. B	**124.** B	**136.** C
113. C	**125.** A	**137.** B
114. C	**126.** D	**138.** A
115. B	**127.** B	**139.** A
116. A	**128.** C	**140.** B
117. A	**129.** A	

RARE

141. A	**146.** B	**151.** C
142. B	**147.** B	**152.** B
143. A	**148.** C	**153.** A
144. C	**149.** C	**154.** E
145. C	**150.** A	**155.** A

156. B	175. C	194. B
157. C	176. B	195. C
158. C	177. C	196. C
159. A	178. B	197. A
160. B	179. A	198. B
161. C	180. A	199. A
162. C	181. B	200. B
163. A	182. B	201. C
164. C	183. B	202. A
165. A	184. B	203. B
166. C	185. A	204. A
167. A	186. A	205. B
168. B	187. C	206. C
169. A	188. C	207. A
170. C	189. A	208. A
171. B	190. A	209. C
172. B	191. A	210. B
173. A	192. A	
174. A	193. B	

EPIC

211. B	227. B	244. B
212. A	228. A	245. B
213. A	229. C	246. A
214. C	230. C	247. A
215. A	231. A	248. C
216. C	232. A	249. B
217. B	233. B	250. A
218. A	234. C	251. A
219. C	235. B	252. B
220. 1:A, 2:D, 3:B, 4:C	236. B	253. C
	237. A	254. B
221. A	238. A, E & F	255. B
222. A	239. B	256. A
223. C	240. A	257. B
224. C	241. B	258. C
225. A	242. C	259. A
226. B	243. A	260. B

261. A	268. A	275. B
262. C	269. B	276. C
263. A	270. A	277. A
264. B	271. C	278. A
265. B	272. A	279. B
266. C	273. A	280. B
267. B	274. B	

LEGENDARY

281. C	291. C	301. C
282. B	292. A	302. B
283. A	293. C	303. C
284. B	294. A	304. B
285. A & E	295. B	305. A
286. A	296. B	306. B
287. C	297. B	307. C
288. C	298. B	308. B
289. B	299. A	309. C
290. A	300. A	310. B

311. A	**331.** B	
312. C	**332.** C	
313. B	**333.** A	
314. C	**334.** A	
315. A	**335.** C	
316. A	**336.** B	
317. B	**337.** B	
318. A	**338.** C	
319. A	**339.** A	
320. A	**340.** A	
321. B	**341.** B	
322. A	**342.** B	
323. C	**343.** C	
324. C	**344.** C	
325. B	**345.** A	
326. A	**346.** A	
327. B	**347.** B	
328. A	**348.** A	
329. C	**349.** A	
330. A	**350.** B	